RASTAFARIAN

© 1988 Watts Books
Paperback edition 1995

Watts Books
96 Leonard Street
London
EC2A 4RH

Franklin Watts Australia
14 Mars Road
Lane Cove
N.S.W. 2066

UK ISBN: 0 86313 675 3 (hardback)
UK ISBN: 0 7496 2271 7 (paperback)

Dewey Decimal Classification Number 299

Design: Edward Kinsey

Typesetting: Tradespools Ltd

Printed by G. Canale, Turin, Italy

The Publishers would like to thank the Gaynor family and all other people shown in this book.

Obadiah (Lloyd Robinson), was President of the Birmingham branch of the Ethiopian World Federation 1981–5.

Note: Many of the photographs in this book originally appeared in 'My Belief: I am a Rastafarian'.

RASTAFARIAN

Jenny Wood

Photographs: Chris Fairclough
Consultant: Obadiah

Watts Books
London/New York/Sydney

These people are Rastafarians.
They follow a way of life
that has come to be called Rastafari.

Rastafari has many links with the Christian and Jewish faiths. Rastafarians study the Bible, especially the Old Testament.

Rastafari was begun in Jamaica
in the 1920s by Marcus Garvey.
He said that an African king
would save and help black people.

HAILE SELASSIE I
Emperor of Ethiopia

Emperor Haile Selassie I of Ethiopia
was crowned in 1930.
He was seen as the African king.
Rastafarians call him Jah
and worship him as God.

Rastafarians are guided by
the culture of Ethiopia.
Their colours are those
of the Ethiopian flag.

Rastafarians are taught
never to cut their hair,
as it is a symbol of strength.
The long braids are called dreadlocks.

Women always keep
their hair covered.
Men uncover it at Meetings.

Rastafarians usually wear ordinary clothes.
African clothes are made for special occasions.

On Holy Days, white clothes are often worn as well as the traditional Rastafarian knitted hat, called a tam.

Rastafarians do not always have
churches or special buildings
to meet in. They may have
their weekly Meeting
in a local community hall.

Meetings are led by the Chaplain.
He is elected for one year,
and has special duties
such as visiting the sick.

There is always music
at the weekly Meetings.
Drummers accompany
the hymns and songs.

The Meetings always begin
with the Ethiopian National Anthem.

Rastafarians hold their hands
in a special way when they pray,
to represent a heart and a spear,
the symbols of peace and war.

After the hymns and prayers,
there is a Business Meeting
to plan everyday duties
and special events.

Most Rastafarians do not eat meat.
Many do not eat fish, eggs
or dairy foods. They like to buy
fresh vegetables and fruit.

Rastafarians believe that
a healthy diet is an important part
of a healthy lifestyle.

Rastafarian music is called reggae. Through reggae, Rastafarians sing about their beliefs and their lives.

Arts and crafts are important
to Rastafarians. They make objects
from natural materials
such as wood and coconut shells.

Rastafarians enjoy spending time with their family and friends. They hold many family festivals when the whole community meets to celebrate their way of life.

FACTS ABOUT RASTAFARIANS

The Rastafari movement was started in Jamaica in the 1920s by Marcus Garvey, a black leader.

Before he became Emperor, Haile Selassie's name was Ras Tafari. The Rastafarian faith is named after him.

Rastafarians believe in:
– one true God, Haile Selassie I of Ethiopia
– that they will all return to Africa, their true home
– that black people will be free

Rastafarians believe that Jah came to Earth in human form as Emperor Haile Selassie I of Ethiopia in Africa. He was a black king who came to help black people whose ancestors had been taken from Africa by slave traders.

Rastafari is a way of life, not a religion but it has many links with the Christian and Jewish faiths.

GLOSSARY

Chaplain
The person who leads the weekly Meeting.

Dreadlocks
The long, uncombed hair of Rastafarians.

Haile Selassie I
He was crowned Emperor of Ethiopia in 1930. Rastafarians believe he was Jah in human form.

Jah
The Rastafarian name for God.

National Anthem
The song or hymn of a country which is sung or played on special occasions.

Ras Tafari
Haile Selassie's name before he became Emperor. "Ras" means prince or head, and "Tafari" means creator.

Reggae
A type of music which began in Jamaica.

Tam
A traditional Rastafarian knitted hat.

INDEX